In Session with Charlie Parker

AF085271

Faber Music

The copying of © copyright material is a criminal offence and may lead to prosecution.

Series Editor: Sadie Cook

Music Transcription: Mike Williams
Recorded by Mike Williams (alto/tenor saxophones), Simon Purcell (piano), Amy Baldwin (double bass) and Dave Wickins (drums)
Music Editorial & Project Management: Artemis Music Limited

© International Music Publications Ltd
First published by International Music Publications Ltd in 1999
International Music Publications Ltd is a Faber Music company
Brownlow Yard, 12 Roger Street, London WC1N 2JU

Cover Photo: Michael Ochs Archives
All photos supplied by Redferns Music Picture Library
Design & Production: Space DPS Limited
Printed in England by Caligraving Ltd
All rights reserved

ISBN10: 0-571-52598-9
EAN13: 978-0-571-52598-0

Reproducing this music in any form is illegal and forbidden by the Copyright, Designs and Patents Act, 1988

To buy Faber Music publications or to find out about the full range of titles available, please contact your local music retailer or Faber Music sales enquiries:

Faber Music Ltd, Burnt Mill, Elizabeth Way, Harlow, CM20 2HX England
Tel: +44(0)1279 82 89 82
fabermusic.com

In Session with Charlie Parker

In the Book...

Introduction 4

Notes on the Solo Analysis . . 8

Billie's Bounce 10

Ornithology 15

Yardbird Suite 22

Now's The Time 27

Donna Lee 34

Anthropology 42

 To download the online audio scan the QR code or go to fabermusic.com/audio.

Track **1**   Tuning Tones

Billie's Bounce
Track **2**   Fast tempo with saxophone
Track **3**   Fast tempo backing track
Track **4**   Slow tempo with saxophone
Track **5**   Slow tempo backing track

Ornithology
Track **6**   Fast tempo with saxophone
Track **7**   Fast tempo backing track
Track **8**   Slow tempo with saxophone
Track **9**   Slow tempo backing track

Yardbird Suite
Track **10**   Fast tempo with saxophone
Track **11**   Fast tempo backing track
Track **12**   Slow tempo with saxophone
Track **13**   Slow tempo backing track

Now's The Time
Track **14**   Fast tempo with saxophone
Track **15**   Fast tempo backing track
Track **16**   Slow tempo with saxophone
Track **17**   Slow tempo backing track

Donna Lee
Track **18**   Fast tempo with saxophone
Track **19**   Fast tempo backing track
Track **20**   Slow tempo with saxophone
Track **21**   Slow tempo backing track

Anthropology
Track **22**   Fast tempo with saxophone
Track **23**   Fast tempo backing track
Track **24**   Slow tempo with saxophone
Track **25**   Slow tempo backing track

Biography

Take a few narcotics, add in a pinch of alcohol, stir in some cultural tension fuelled by a new and dangerous music; now add prohibition, a tragically shortened life and a musical gift as prodigious as it was revolutionary. Now you have the basic ingredients for the life story of one of the greatest and most influential jazz musicians ever – Charlie 'Bird' Parker.

He was born in Kansas City on 29th August 1920, the only son of Charles and Addie Parker. He started learning the baritone sax but found his true instrument when his mother gave him an alto sax. Such was his infatuation with the instrument that at the age of 14 he dropped out of school completely to dedicate himself to it. He got the nickname 'Yardbird' from his love of chicken. This inelegant sobriquet was subsequently shortened to the altogether more appealing 'Bird', and it stuck.

His first forays into the world of the professional jazz musician were anything but successful, however. Kansas City musicians were very competitive (Herschel Evans and Ben Webster both came from Kansas) and if you couldn't cut it, you were out! On Parker's first time out, at the High Hat Club, he dried up half way through a solo on *Body And Soul* and didn't touch the instrument for three months afterwards. A potentially more damaging later outing culminated in drummer Jo Jones throwing a cymbal at Parker as a subtle way of telling him to get off the stage! Rather than discouraging him this experience seemed to stiffen Bird's resolve, as he simply practised more diligently and for longer hours than he had before.

He started to get regular work, first with Tommy Douglas (1936-7) and then with Buster Smith (1937-8). At this time he started to study harmony with pianist Carrie Powell, a move that laid the first brick in the impressive wall of his mastery of jazz improvisation.

In 1938 he joined the band of Jay McShann, and started to make a name for himself as a hard-swinging taker-of-liberties with jazz harmony.

In 1939 he made his first visit to New York, where he was greatly influenced by the musical style of the Big Apple. It was during his time with McShann that he made his first recordings (in 1941). These early recordings (including *Sepian Bounce*, *Jumpin' Blues* and *Lonely Boy Blues*) brought him to the attention of a wider jazz public, and his reputation as a harmonic innovator began to spread.

Photo: William Gottlieb

Charlie Parker

Photo: William Gottlieb

During the Second World War he hooked up with Earl Hines (1942-3) and Billy Eckstine (1944) where he met Dizzy Gillespie, a prodigious young trumpeter with a cutting sound and an attitude to match.

In 1942 Bird moved to New York where, with a variety of musicians including Dizzy and drummers Kenny Clarke and Max Roach, and with Thelonious Monk on piano, he helped pioneer bebop.

By 1945 bebop had caught the nation's attention from its New York spiritual home, and Parker was by this time leading his own outfit. A West Coast residency at Billy Berg's helped widen the appeal of his music. In 1946 he played at the LA Philharmonic, and in the same year he cut a number of landmark recordings for the Dial record label.

During all this time Parker had been living up to his 'rabble rouser' image, with a growing record of narcotic and alcohol abuse, which culminated in the famous 'Loverman session' incident in 1946 when, after a recording session he was so desperate that he set light to his hotel room.

A spell in the psychiatric wing of the LA county jail was the consequence of that affair, followed by six months rehab, which Bird ironically celebrated in the recording RELAXIN' AT CAMARILLO in 1947.

When he returned to normal life he immediately set to work recording for Dial, this time with Erroll Garner. The appeal of New York proved irresistible and in 1947 he returned to form a band with the hot young trumpet sensation Miles Davis and drummer Max Roach. It was with this band that Parker arguably hit his peak.

1949 saw Parker touring a foreign country for the first time when he played the Paris festival, following that with a trip to Scandinavia in 1950.

In the same year, and in an attempt to reach a wider audience, he released an album of music with string orchestra, and the success of this venture led to a number of dates with this line-up. However, Bird thrived on the cut and thrust of a challenging improvisatory dialogue, something this sanitised, unashamedly populist style of music couldn't supply.

> "Music is your own experience, your thoughts, your wisdom. If you don't live it, it won't come out on your horn."
>
> Charlie Parker.

The definitive Parker recordings were made for two labels during the mid to late 40s: on Savoy between 1945-8 he recorded *Now's The Time*, *Thriving On A Riff* and *Billie's Bounce*, and for Dial between 1946-7 he recorded *Ornithology*, *A Night In Tunisia*, *Lover Man* and *Scrapple From The Apple*.

His last public appearance was in 1955 at Birdland, the club named after him, but it was not an auspicious finale. He rowed publicly with pianist Bud Powell, who stormed off stage, quickly followed by bassist Charlie Mingus. Depressed, disillusioned, his body wasted by disease and years of abuse, Bird sought solace with the great patron and friend of bebop, Baroness de Koenigswater. Eight days after that fateful gig he was found dead in her hotel suite.

Musical Style

Parker's interests and influences were as diverse and far-reaching as one could imagine – from the classical sophistication of Hindemith and Stravinsky to the primitive directness of the Kansas City blues tradition, which Parker was immersed in from his upbringing and early professional employment with the Jay McShann Orchestra, of which he was a conscientious lead alto player.

As an intelligent and deeply sensitive man, he lived through the whole panorama of human emotions from joy and love, through to tragedy and despair – and it's all here in his playing.

His conception of sound was based on that of the altoist Buster Smith, and the leading tenor saxophone player of the day Lester 'Pres' Young, whose comparatively vibrato-less sound was adopted by Bird on the alto saxophone. Parker says of 'Pres', 'I was crazy about Lester, he played so clean and beautifully'.

Although Parker completely overhauled Lester's harmonic and rhythmic concepts, he had indeed transcribed and memorised much of the tenor star's recorded output with the Count Basie Band, and as the formative bebop drummer Kenny Clarke relates: 'We went to listen to Bird at Monroe's, for no other reason except that he sounded like 'Pres', until we found out that he had something of his own to offer, something new'.

> "Bird's mind and fingers work with incredible speed. He can imply four chord changes in a melodic pattern where another musician would have trouble inserting two."
>
> Leonard Feather.

That 'something new' was a melodic appreciation of the upper extensions of conventional chord progressions and cadences which Bird had been practising at jam sessions with the guitarist Biddy Fleet. As Parker himself explains: 'Well that night I was working over *Cherokee*, and as I did I found that by using the higher intervals of the chord as a melody line, and backing them with appropriately related changes, I could play the thing I'd been hearing – I came alive.'

This explanation from the saxophonist is both clear and informative, but it fails to do justice to the depth of his innovation, which included chromaticisation of melody and harmonic introduction of passing chords, chord substitution, displacement of the harmonic metre and, on occasion, extensive reharmonisation. When you combine this with an awe-inspiring rhythmic approach, containing complete freedom of accentuation and articulation, you have the musical personality who went on to revolutionise concepts of small group playing on every instrument.

While not wishing to devalue Parker's greatness or individual achievement, he was part of an extraordinarily fertile musical environment amongst an expanding circle of young musicians, whose daring and musical exploration were leading them down similar roads of enquiry.

The nightly jam sessions at Minton's Playhouse in New York provided the focal point for this group, which included Thelonious Monk, Charlie Christian, Dizzy Gillespie and Kenny Clarke amongst others. It was at such venues that the small group, consisting of two or three frontline and rhythm section, began to assert its ascendancy over the larger ensembles of the swing era as the preferred working environment for the serious improviser.

Photo: William Gottlieb

CHARLIE PARKER discography

Here is a guide to suggested listening for each of the pieces in this book:

'Billie's Bounce' – 26/11/45, New York City – The Charlie Parker Re-boppers – The Complete Savoy Sessions – with Miles Davis (tpt), Sadik Hakim (pno), Curly Russell (bass), Max Roach (drums) Savoy/Arista 5850-1

'Ornithology' – 24/12/49 – Carnegie Hall, New York City – with Red Rodney (tpt), Al Haig (pno), Tommy Potter (bass), Roy Haynes (drums), S.C.A.M. JPG1

'Yardbird Suite' - 28/3/46 – with Miles Davis (tpt), 'Lucky' Thompson (tenor sax), Arv Garrison (gtr), Dodo Marmorosa (pno), Viv McMillan (bass), Roy Porter (drums) – released on 'Bird Symbols' – Atlantic Music Corporation 407

'Now's the Time' – 24/12/49 – Carnegie Hall, New York City – with Red Rodney (tpt), Al Haig (pno), Tommy Potter (bass), Roy Haynes (drums) S.C.A.M. JPG1

'Donna Lee' – 8/5/47 – The Charlie Parker All Stars – The Complete Savoy Sessions – with Miles Davis (tpt), Bud Powell (pno), Tommy Potter (bass), Max Roach (drums) Savoy/Arista 3420-2

'Anthropology' – 3/5/49 – Radio Broadcast, Royal Roost Night Club, New York City – with Charlie Parker, Kenny Dorham (tpt), Al Haig (pno), 'Lucky' Thompson (tenor sax), Milt Jackson (vibraphone), Tommy Potter (bass), Max Roach (drums)

Bird's style is the culmination of the musical developments of the experiments of the early 1940s, taking in the harmonic knowledge of the great pianist Art Tatum and giants of the saxophone such as Don Byas and Coleman Hawkins, all delivered with incredible virtuosity and the raw passion of the blues.

Performance Notes

Billie's Bounce
This is one of two blues compositions in this selection and is an ideal starting point for any saxophone player who wants to get to grips with Parker's style. This is a comparatively short solo (see if you can memorise it) and shows how Bird was able to tailor his playing to the demands of any situation.

Ornithology
The theme of *Ornithology* was originally a phrase Parker improvised on Jay McShann's *The Jumping Blues*, which Benny Harris crafted over the chord progression of the standard *How High The Moon*, a common variant of the 32-bar song format ABAC (4 x 8-bar phrases). This 'Carnegie Hall' performance bears all of Parker's trademarks – for example, fantastic singing sound, time feeling, varied articulation and an indefiable sense of structure allied to form.

Yardbird Suite
'Yardbird' was one of Charlie Parker's nicknames, derived from his liking for fried chicken. This composition, with its rigorous functional harmony and modulation to the key of III minor in the bridge, records the saxophonist's agility and succinctness of phrasing over chord changes and his understanding and mastery of the 32-bar song form.

Now's The Time
Jay McShann (one of Parker's first musical employers) considered his protégé to be the greatest of blues players, and while such comparative terms are ultimately meaningless in any discussion of the human spirit, we can perhaps forgive McShann for getting carried away in this case. This performance of the blues, over six majestically constructed choruses, illustrates Parker's depth of connection to and understanding of this most archetypal of forms.

Donna Lee
Although credited to Parker, there is a strong suspicion amongst musicians that this 'line' over the chord progression of *Indiana*, was actually penned by the young trumpeter Miles Davis, who spent much of his formative period as the saxophonist's sideman. If this is indeed the case, then the tune is a classic example of how Parker's vocabulary was identified and applied by his contemporaries.

Anthropology
This is a daring virtuosic performance at 'break–neck' tempo of a Parker 'line' over the chord progression of *I Got Rhythm* (which musicians now refer to as 'rhythm' changes). These changes have been a stalwart of many jazz players up to and including the present day. With its rapidly moving harmony, albeit within tonic and subdominant key areas, and its cyclic middle eight (III^7 / / / | / / / / | VI^7 / / / | / / / / | II^7 / / / | / / / / | V^7 / / / | / / / / ||) it remains a challenge to contemporary improvisers.

Charlie Parker

Notes on the Solo Analysis

It will help us enormously in our appraisal of Parker's playing if we can gain insight into how his note choices function within the melodic line.

To illustrate this, we will examine three extracts in the following terms:
1. Chord notes – the 1, 3, 5, 7 of the chord
2. Passing notes – a note or notes that pass between two chord notes
3. Neighbour notes – the four notes which are a tone and semi-tone above and below a chord note.

Ex 1

This is bars 22 and 23 of the solo from *Billie's Bounce*. The A♮ in bar 23 is a chord note of D^7 (the 5th) and is the destination (or target) of the notes in bar 22. The B, B♭ and A♭ respectively constitute the upper neighbour note, the chromatic upper neighbour note, and the chromatic lower neighbour notes to the A♮, and serve to draw the ear to the resolution on to the 5th of the chord.

In bar 23, the A (5th), F♯ (3rd) and D (root) are obviously all chord notes of D^7. The G passes between two chord notes, F♯ and A, and is therefore a passing note. The B♮ in bar 22 is a neighbour note to the A in bar 23. Whilst appreciating that the B♮ is the 13th of D^7, it is also useful to realise that 13ths derive much of their particular quality from their relationship with the 5th.

Ex 2

The above example is bars 32–33 (the solo break) from *Ornithology*. The B♮ in bar 33 is the 5th of E major and is the target for the A, C♮ and B♭ which 'prepare' and lead the ear to it. Again, whilst appreciating that the C♮ is the ♭9 of B^7, the main question to ask is how does the note function in terms of the melodic phrase?

The G♮ in bar 33 is the lower chromatic neighbour note to the G♯ (the 3rd of E major). Notice that the D♯ and F♯ (the 7th and 9th of E major) are lower and upper neighbour notes to the root of E. The 7th and 9th of chords derive their particular quality from their relationship with the root, and in the case of the 9th the 3rd also.

The descending D♯ and C♯ – which pass between E and B (chord notes) – are, in this system, passing notes. You will notice that the same note can have more than one melodic function, depending on what precedes and follows it.

Ex 3

In the above example (bars 116–117 of *Anthropology*), the C♯ and B♭ in bar 116 are both neighbour notes to the 5th of E^7 (B♮). The second C♯ still functions as a neighbour note to B♮, although the B♮ is not sounded again until the beginning of the next bar. An important point about neighbour notes is that they don't *have* to be resolved and, alternatively, the resolution can be delayed, as here. Note that when the B♮ (the destination of the descending phrase in bar 116) is played at the beginning of bar 117, it is now the 9th of A^7 instead of the 5th of A^7.

The E♭ in bar 116 is a chromatic passing note, coming as it does between two chord notes – the root and the 7th of E^7: E and D.

As we reiterate later in the book, Parker accesses this kind of detail and beauty intuitively. That is to say, he wasn't thinking in these terms during performance, he was hearing it. Even with this brief introduction, it is helpful for us to think about phrasing in the way that the ear hears it – in terms of tension and release rather than attempting to justify Parker's chromatic choices in relation to chord/scale theory. That is not to say that this approach replaces chord/scale theory, rather it complements it. For the musician who wishes to explore this further, a study of Schenkerian analysis is recommended.

In relation to the solos described in this book, this approach will help to shed light on why certain things sound so good and, most obviously, to understand Parker's use of chromaticism.

Playing Guide

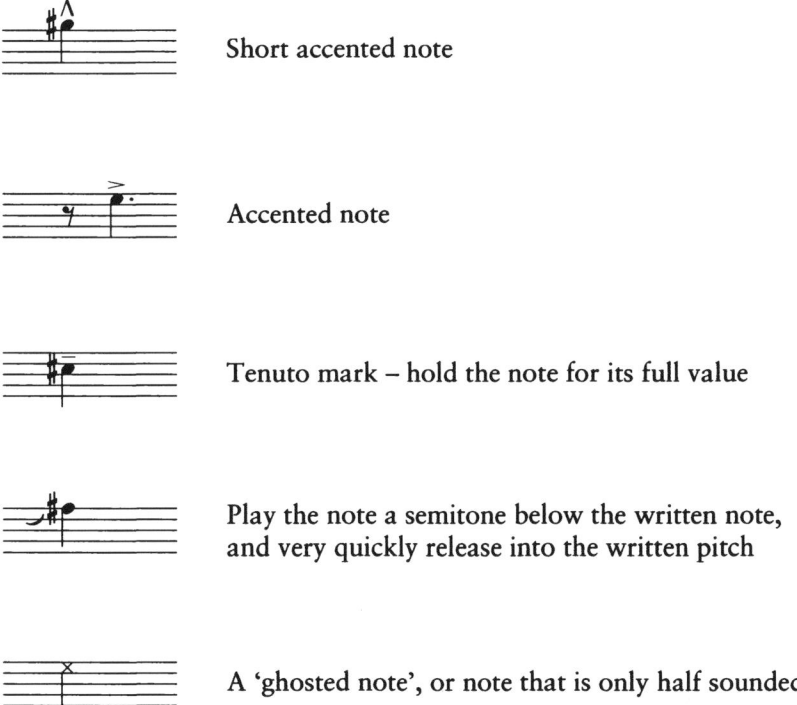

Short accented note

Accented note

Tenuto mark – hold the note for its full value

Play the note a semitone below the written note, and very quickly release into the written pitch

A 'ghosted note', or note that is only half sounded

Charlie Parker

BILLIE'S BOUNCE

By Charlie Parker

The Solo

Billie's Bounce

Within the three choruses, the ideas unfold naturally and in balance with each other. The beginning of the second chorus expands the opening phrase of the first in much the same way as people mull over and return to themes in a conversation.

Ex 1

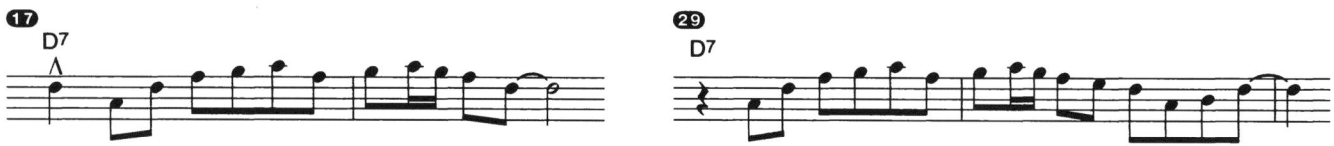

Bar 23 returns to the motif in bar 18, which itself is developed further in bars 41 and 42.

Ex 2

In each of these examples the phrase returns on a different rhythmic placement of the bar. Also see bars 33 and 34 which re-invent the ascending quaver triplet phrase from bars 26 and 27, and bar 42 which is reinforced by bar 45.

TECHNIQUE tip

At medium tempos, a basic requirement of the music is to be able to feel beats 2 and 4 of each bar, as the rhythmic anchor of the solo. Giving this obvious aspect of your playing some attention, both in your practise and listening time, will help to develop rhythmic confidence and understanding of the idiom.

This repetition and, importantly, development of material raises an enormously valuable musical issue for us as improvisers – that is, it's not necessarily how many ideas you come up with, but how you work with and expand the ideas you do have and in how many different ways and contexts you can apply them.

Harmonically, we have the usual selection of bounties that Parker regularly serves up – so we have unadulterated blues playing in bar 21 and bars 41–46, in combination with gems of phrasing (bars 24 and 36) which simultaneously describe the cadence points and which are individual melodic statements in their own right.

Ex 3

Bar 22 (and 23) which is shown in the example above, contains highly detailed chromatic tension and release within the line (see 'Notes on the Solo Analysis') as does

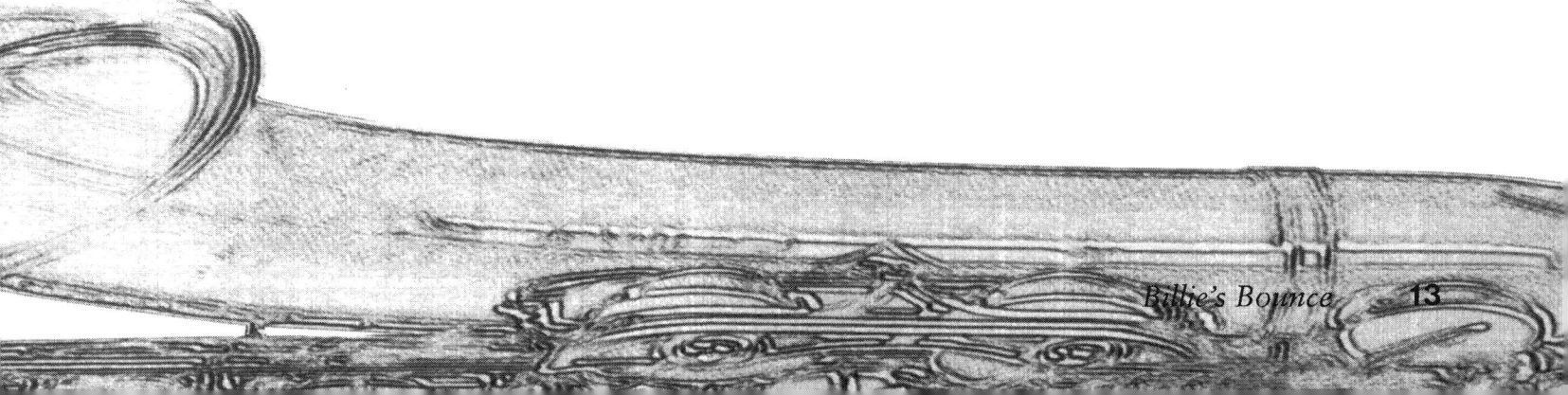

bar 19. The accentuation of the 7th of the D^7 chord, prepares the move to the subdominant – a favourite melodic trait of Parker. The subtlety of the man is evident in the way he uses the tonic (D), initially to bring his first chorus to a conclusion and then to launch the beginning of the next, re-iterating the truth that clarity and simplicity are usually indicative of the greatest intelligence, musical or otherwise.

Practice Tip

Take some of the melodic phrases from this solo and see if you can use the material as a starting point to compose your own blues head and/or solo. Don't be afraid to return to phrases you've already used (this is part of the vocal tradition of the blues anyway – that is, to make a statement, to make it again, and then to comment on it). In this way you will naturally begin to assimilate the language of Parker, and will be mirroring the way he learnt (amongst many of the older generation of players). You will also be practising material from this performance in a creative way.

ORNITHOLOGY

By Charlie Parker and Bennie Harris

Ornithology

The Solo

Ornithology

It is an interesting exercise to sing the melody of *How High The Moon* over Bird's solo here, because it becomes apparent that far from obscuring the melody the solo actually functions as an elaborate counterpoint.

One of the reasons Parker's music communicates so directly is the completeness of his melodic statements which he expertly frames with space, allowing himself and the music to breathe (bars 36 and 40). Alternatively, he may follow a seemingly fully self-contained idea with a complementary and/or satirical afterthought, such as that which appears in bar 44 (as in all great art there is an in-built sense of proportion and perspective, and internal balance).

Throughout the solo Bird uses chromaticism to embellish the line, which further energises his playing with the resulting in-built tension and release (see bars 33, 37, 45, 50 and so on); the use of the $V^{7(\flat 9)}$ shape (bar 32 and bars 42 and 46 amongst others); and strong descriptive and melodic chord shapes, utilising 7ths and 9ths (for example bars 33, 38, 39, 41 and 48 to name but a few).

Bars 49–57 show Parker taking one melodic idea and adapting it to effect, in this case the modulation to D major. In this instance – bars 51 and 52 – he alters the given harmony:

| Em^7 / / / | A^7 / / / | Dmaj / / / | Dmaj / / / ||

which he embellishes with:

| Em^7 / Em-maj^7 | Em / A^7 / | Dmaj / / / | Dmaj / / / ||

Bird then exploits the inner line of root, major 7th, minor 7th–3rd.

Ex 1

This became a favourite harmonic device of the bebop generation players such as Sonny Rollins, Sonny Stitt, Kenny Dorham and so on.

Bars 64 and 65 are interesting for their use of the B^{7+} chord and the way Bird decorates the ensuing line of the $9\text{-}(^{\flat}13)\text{-}(9)$.

Ex 2

Bar 65 is also interesting for its use of the melodic quality of the unresolved major 7th.

Bars 74 – 78 utilise a three-note grouping/interval structure of a semitone then a tritone.

Ex 3

Bird transposes the structure through the chord progression, a concept used by many contemporary improvisers who, since Coltrane, have explored this territory extensively. Parker may have conceived of this idea from his studies of Slonimsky's *Thesaurus of Scales and Melodic Patterns*, which retains its relevance as a research resource.

Practice Tip

The main rhythmic constituent of Parker's solo (and the melody) is the quaver or eighth note, so we must be able to deliver the phrases in a way that ignites the rhythmic vitality of the solo. Parker achieves this through the quality of support he maintains for the air stream at all times, which allows him to accent, and inversely to 'ghost' (or de-emphasise) certain parts of phrases. In bar 6 of the melody the F♮ is accented to enhance the syncopation of its rhythmic placement in the bar (notice Ray Haynes' bass drum push here in conjunction with this) and the D♮ and B♭ in bar 8 are both subtly inflected to give them more emphasis. Throughout the solo be aware of how you attack and end notes, and where you accent within phrases. This will help bring the music alive for you. (Parker's language is as much a rhythmic conception as it is a harmonic one.)

A good way of practising this approach is to take a phrase you're working on at a slower tempo and play it through without tonguing so that you're relying on the air-stream alone for the projection of each note. The next step is to experiment with accents – firstly using the support from the abdomen and secondly by introducing the tongue. Once you can make all the notes speak with an even quality of sound across the registers you can use your tongue to accent, attack and inflect notes to good effect. Stylistically this is essential to the music because it is part of the rhythmic dialogue across the whole band – that is, there is interplay between the snare and bass drum accents and the piano comping, accents in the bass line and the soloistic statements.

A good tip here is to refer to the original recording and to learn to sing some of the phrases (or the whole solo if you like), so that you begin to 'internalise' the music. Remember that the sound you hear in your head and feel in your heart is what ultimately comes out of the horn, as much as any saxophone/mouthpiece/reed permutation. If you are having difficulty at any time, for instance with a particular phrase, practise it in the same way as you would a technical exercise. Think of it as a musical investment you can't fail to cash in on.

TECHNIQUE tip

Use of the 'Bis key' for the B♭ fingerings is recommended throughout.

Yardbird Suite

By Charlie Parker

© 1946 Atlantic Music. © renewed and assigned 1974 Atlantic Music Corp, USA
This arrangement © 1999
All rights for UK and Eire by Marada Music Ltd, London W14 0LJ

The Solo

Yardbird Suite

This is a miniature masterpiece of construction over just one chorus, and demonstrates the intuitive compositional mind of a great improviser. It is no coincidence that the first two statements of the solo are exactly the same length – 3 ½ beats – with identical rhythmic stress.

Ex 1

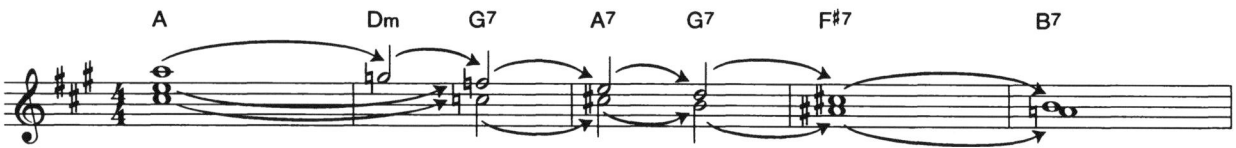

The first four bars of this solo demonstrate the kind of detail and balance Parker was capable of manipulating 'off the cuff'. The notes written in Example 1 are the key points of the phrase (bars 36–40) which the ear is led to melodically. Incidentally the tune of 'Yardbird' establishes the top line here, but in the solo Parker embellishes both of these lines simultaneously, as well as a hint at the root movement in bar 38 – via the A on the last quaver of bar 37 and in bar 39 – melodic exploitation of the line ♯9 - ♭9 - 5th. When we arrive at bar 40, the logical continuation of the upper line would be to descend to the root of the II^7 chord – B^7 – which is why the C♯, which contradicts this prepared expectation, gets the maximum from its quality as the unresolved 9th. This all sounds incredibly academic, and it is important to remember that most of this detail was accessed intuitively. On the other hand, this kind of cognitive appreciation can often 'kick start' the intuition into gear. It can't be a bad thing to consider why, and how, something sounds great!

In bars 42 and 43 Parker went on to use this phrase as a 'riff' blues head entitled *Cool Blues*.

Ex 2

Here the root movement is melodically embellished within the line, and bars 46 and 47 are unified by the ascending semitone to firstly emphasise the G and secondly the F♯.

Ex 3

The above example details the descending line inherent in bars 45-47 as already shown in example 2.

Ex 4

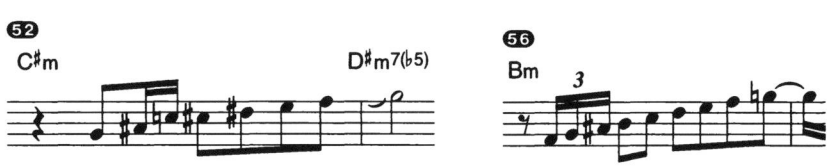

Yardbird Sute 25

In the bridge of this solo bar 56 transposes the contour of the phrase at bar 52 down a tone from C♯ minor to B minor.

Bar 58 reinforces the 'gesture' of Bar 57. Subtly, Bird waits to resolve the A♯ in bar 57 until bar 59.

These examples show Parker making a mockery of the difficulties contained in the chord progression and they result in a highly organised compositional statement over 32 bars.

Instrumentally speaking, Parker's playing here uses traces of vibrato in the sound in what, for him, is quite an unusual way. As a saxophonist he was one of the first, after his original model Lester Young, to curtail the use of vibrato and to use it more discerningly, in a very vocal way. In this solo the delicacy and finesse of Parker's sound counter-balances perfectly the invincibility of his musical thought process.

TECHNIQUE tip

Maintaining the dynamic and support right to the end of each phrase maximises its impact and infuses the space with expectancy and swing.

Practice Tip

Begin by singing the A section of the melody, and then move on to singing the 'lines' in Example 1. Have a go at vocally improvising round the line and then repeat the whole procedure with the saxophone. This can be a lot of fun and will help you get inside the phrasing and delivery of the A sections of Parker's solo. You can practise this approach as an improvisational resource in any context you choose.

Now's The Time

By Charlie Parker

Now's The Time

The Solo

Now's The Time

This is an audacious offering from the saxophone player, containing some of his most celebrated and oft-quoted vocabulary (see bars 26–30, bars 34 and 35, and bars 54–56. Throughout, the performance is littered with the most poignant of blues proclamations which remarkably transform relatively simple musical resources into the most strident and meaningful of deliveries (for example bars 37 and 38). This is achieved through an incredible understanding and respect for the tradition that gave rise to this music, backed up by virtuosic instrumental command of articulation and inflection.

Over the six choruses there is an identifiable pattern to the organisation of material which is self-evident, that is, while the harmony remains more static (for example, in bars 1–6 of each chorus on the tonic and sub-dominant chords), the phrasing is more vocal and drawn out.

Bird saves his more explosive double-time passages for bars 7–12 of each chorus, where we have the bebop generation's harmonic adaptations to the blues for which Parker was very much responsible. For example, from bar 7 of the chorus:

(7) (8) (9) (10) (11) (12)

| IIImi / VI^7 / | ♭IIIm^7 / ♭VI^7 / | IImi^7 / / / | V^7 / / / | I / VI^7 / | IImi / V^7 ||

Here the phrasing is more descriptive of the shifting harmony.

Before we leave this solo, bar 52 is interesting because Bird intimates at the tritone substitute of D^7 which is A♭^{7}.

Ex 1

Unusually, however, he does this in bar 3 of the chorus. This is interesting because it was more conventional, and still is, to insert the tritone substitution in bar 4 of the blues, in this case $A^{\flat 7}$– G^7. Bars 63 and 64 are interesting because Bird implies the harmony of $E^{\flat 7}$. With the $^\flat II^7$ chord functioning as the tritone dominant of D^7 (that is, the tritone substitute of the dominant of D^7– A^7),

(62)   (63)   (64)

| D^7 / / / | $E^{\flat 7\sharp 11}$ / / / | $E^{\flat 7}$ / D^7 / | D^7 / / /

Ex 2

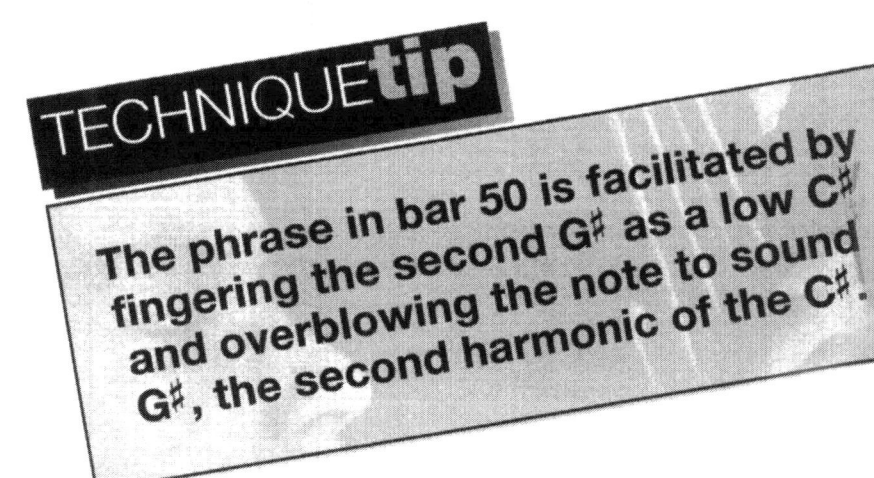

these are harmonic principles that have subsequently become major roads of inquiry for many of the players at the forefront of the music.

TECHNIQUE tip

The phrase in bar 50 is facilitated by fingering the second G♯ as a low C♯ and overblowing the note to sound G♯, the second harmonic of the C♯.

Practice Tip

When practising this piece, see if you can really get inside the more blues-orientated phrases, and deliver them as if you were singing! As with all these transcriptions, it is essential to check out the original recording, because the inflection and rhythmic placement is so personal, and notation is only the starting point for the music. Jazz is, and always has been, primarily an aural tradition.

Donna Lee

By Charlie Parker

Donna Lee

Donna Lee

The Solo

Donna Lee

Parker's solo contains much of the harmonic information and contour from the actual melody, material which has been assimilated by the tradition because of its enduring melodic strength and harmonic logic. A detailed study of the melody would be beneficial in itself, however, let us concern ourselves here with the Parker solo which contains all of the musical ideas and principles within the original line – and more.

One of the defining aspects of Bird's style as opposed to his predecessors who influenced him (for example, Lester Young), was his use of the added notes/extensions in his arpeggiation of the harmony. So for example, as we have already seen elsewhere, he arpeggiates the $V^{7(\flat 9)}$ chords from the 3rd of the $V^{7(\flat 9)}$ chord (superimposing a resulting diminished 7th shape) in bars 34, 39, 50, 55, 58, 66, 76, 82 and 90.

Likewise, he arpeggiates the G^9 from the 3rd to the natural 9 (superimposing the notes B D F A – $Bm^{7(\flat 5)}$ – over G^7). See bars 35, 67 (where Bird paraphrases the melody at the beginning of the second chorus), 77 and 83. Notice that although the material in these examples is essentially the same, his rhythmic permutation and placement in the bar and across the bar line is seemingly endless.

It is here that we come across another favourite device of Parker – altering the harmonic metre of the chord progression so that the resolution is either delayed or brought forward slightly. In bars 38 and 39 the underlying harmony is C^7–F. However, when we arrive at the F chord, Bird is still outlining the $C^{7(\flat 9)}$ chord, thus delaying the arrival of the tonic chord.

Ex 1

Similarly in bar 55, the stated harmony is Dm^7, but Bird is outlining the $V^{7(\flat 9)}$ of Dm^7 which is $A^{7(\flat 9)}$.

Ex 2

When he does finally resolve to the tonic chord (by implication with the $F\sharp$) in bar 56, the harmony of the tune has moved to $A^{7(\flat 9)}$!

Another example is at bar 71 where the $Cm - F^7$ which we are moving to is brought forward by three beats to expand the cadence from I^7 to IVmaj (that is, (Cm) F^7- B♭).

Ex 3

Finally there is the phrase in bar 92, which is anticipating the harmony in bar 93 (the tonic chord of F major).

Donna Lee

The effect of this harmonic displacement is extremely subtle. At the time Bird was doing this, many of the rhythm section players felt that they were in the wrong part of the progression.

The concept of altering the harmonic metre has been exploited ever since Bird, and understanding it will throw some light on many contemporary improvisers, although stylistically they may be very different.

Another of Parker's mannerisms was to chromatically 'fill in' the space of a descending major 3rd interval – for example, in bar 37 between the 9th and the 7th of G minor (A–F), and in bar 92 where he chromatically 'fills in' the major 3rd interval between E and C.

Bar 79 is interesting because of its arpeggiation of the minor chord through the 7th, 9th and 11th.

Ex 4

The phrase then falls to the 5th of $C^{7(\flat 9 \flat 13)}$ via the accented $\flat 13$ of $C^{7(\flat 9 \flat 13)}$. This is a good example of how Parker could decorate a guide tone line, in this case $\flat 9 - \flat 13 - 5$. There is an echo of this idea in bar 94.

Bars 60–61 and bars 95–96 show Parker inserting an $A\flat m^7$ between A minor and G minor to create a string of descending minor 7ths, a favourite device of his.

Other hallmarks of Parker's style include: outlining of the $E^{\flat 7(\sharp 11)}$ chord in bar 42 and the $D^{7(\sharp 11)}$ chord in bar 44; the 'Honeysuckle Rose' motif in bar 38; and the repetition of the phrase at bars 47, 59 and 87.

Throughout the solo Parker decorates the line with chromatic neighbour and passing notes. For example, at bar 94, the $D^\flat$ and $B^\natural$ both target the $C^\natural$ in the following bar and can be thought of respectively as the upper chromatic and lower chromatic neighbour notes to C. Of course Parker didn't think of this when he was performing, and we certainly don't need to. However, it is crucial to understand, either intuitively or cognitively (and preferably both), how notes function within a melodic line. For example, if we immediately think 'What's the major 7th doing over a C^7 chord at bar 94?', then we've missed the point!

The point is, as the great pianist Bill Evans said, 'There are no wrong notes, just wrong resolutions'! Ultimately there are no rules and no right and wrong.

TECHNIQUE tip

If you particularly like a musical idea, transposing it to all keys and all parts of the instrumental range would be enormously beneficial.

Practice Tip

Take some of the recurring material we've examined and practise the different variants as they occur in the solo (for example, bars 35 and 67). When you have the material under your fingers, practise improvising using the shape and then see if you can incorporate it in your own improvisation. Another way of working in this area is to take a bar (for example bar 56) where Bird superimposes a descending $Gm^{7(\flat 5)}$ shape over $A^{7(\flat 9 \flat 13)}$ and resolves it into the 5th of the next chord, Dm^7.

$$\|: A^{7(\flat 9 \flat 13)} \,/\,/\,/\, | \, Dm \,/\,/\,/ \,:\|$$
$$V^7 \quad I$$

Out of context you can then practise the cadence, and see how many different ways of playing the $Gm^{7(\flat 5)}$ shape you can come up with over the $A^{7(\flat 9 \flat 13)}$ chord, and how you can phrase and resolve (or not resolve) out of it. Only do this with ideas and sounds you are attracted to. The intention here is to take Bird's solo as a starting point for our own musical growth and exploration. It is fine to practise Parker's phrases and transpose them to all keys, but where it begins to get exciting is when you start to practise and apply the musical principles behind the phrases!

Anthropology

By Charlie Parker and Dizzy Gillespie

44 *Anthropology*

The Solo

Anthropology
(also known as Thriving From A Riff)

Parker's solo here represents the man at the peak of his immense powers – instrumentally, structurally and imaginatively. The solo contains many examples of Bird's harmonic freedom and progressive approach, and there are concepts contained therein that have been retained and expanded upon ever since. For instance, bar 37 alludes to a possible tritone substitution $D\flat^7$ for G^7, moving to C^7, and the last two beats of bar 82 where $F^{7(\sharp 11)}$ is implied, moving to E^7 ($F^{7(\sharp 11)}$ is the tritone substitute of B^7 – the original harmony here).

Ex 1

Another outstanding example of Bird's forward harmonic thinking is demonstrated by the material in the first two 'A' sections of the second chorus, where he superimposes a string of $V^{7(\flat 9)}$ chords, ultimately moving to chord IV^7. He realises this largely with connecting diminished 7th shapes that describe the implied $V^{7(\flat 9)}$ movements.

Anthropology

Ex 2

Then in bars 62 and 88 we have the insertion of a $\flat\text{IImaj}^7$ chord resolving to the tonic (that is, $A\flat^9$ going to G). The major chord a semitone above the tonic, or chord we are moving to, functions very much like a dominant.

Ex 3

This is a principle he explores further in the B section of the second chorus, where the stated B^7 chord is approached with a C major idea. In bar 107 the insertion of $B\flat$ minor creates a succession of chromatically descending minor 7th chords, implying B minor - E^7- $B\flat$ minor - $E\flat^7$- A minor - D^7, or more simply E^7 (VI^7) $E\flat^7$ ($\flat VI^7$) D^7 (V^7).

Ex 4

A similar idea can be found in bars 119 and 120 where there is description, and therefore implication, of $E\flat^7$ ($\flat VI^7$) shifting to D^7 (V^7).

These harmonic devices, although radical for the time, were ideas that Parker may have been inspired to explore from his exposure to the great pianist Art Tatum and the 'Giant of the tenor saxophone' Coleman 'Bean' Hawkins who were masters at embellishing and expanding upon the existing harmonic content. They may also have reflected his interest and study of classical music. Parker was highly musically aware 'across the board' (note his humourous reference to Chopin's *A major Polonaise* in bars 124–126, and his quotation from Alphonse Picou's celebrated clarinet obligato from *High Society* (bars 97–98). Indeed, Parker was a master of quotation and was able to incorporate the most banal of contemporary themes into his improvisations and produce moments of pathos and/or humour from the satire and social comment that ensued.

> **TECHNIQUE tip**
>
> When the tempo is very fast, being able to *feel* the time in terms of whole bars, rather than individual beats within the bar, can help to retain a sense of space and physical relaxation in your playing and provide increased technical assurance.

In organisational terms, this solo contains much cross-referencing and development of ideas over the duration of three choruses. Thus the phrase in bars 78 and 79 is an echo of the opening phrase of the solo (the C♯ at the end of the phrase may have been accessed by Parker's use of the side D fingering – the authentic fingering for 'high' D, without the octave key).

Parker's stock vocabulary is well represented throughout. It is important to realise that he uses much of this material as a writer uses punctuation, that is, his use of certain phrases is grammatical and, as such, helps the overall structuring of ideas. For example, the classic phrase in bar 35 is repeated an

octave higher to top off the extraordinary fractured line of bars 36 to 40. It appears again in bar 47 and there is a variation of it in bar 103. Bars 110–111 refer back to bars 46–47, but notice how Parker comes in and out of this phrase differently. Likewise, bars 116–118 are a direct lifting of bars 84–86, but in each case the line either side of this contains different material.

It is important to remember the speed of this performance, and that another facet to the repetition of language is that it allows the improviser to think ahead, buying him time.

The bridge of the first chorus illustrates how Parker could take one idea and develop it for an extended period. In this case, the semitone interval is the prevailing musical idea for bars 49–56. (An instrumental note here – you may want to practise bars 49–50 with the long B♭ and the side C fingerings, also using the Bis key B♭ and normal C fingering.)

Practice Tip

Playing fast tempos requires the ability to stay physically relaxed. In terms of fingering, economy of movement and a comfortable hand position are vital. This can be facilitated by increased control of the weaker fingers. For example, over a period of time you may find it useful to 'anchor' the right hand little finger over the E♭ key and the left hand little finger over the G♯ key. Practising slowly, with the intention of not moving the fingers away from these keys and maintaining a relaxed hand position at all times, will begin to facilitate economy of movement and increased co-ordination and accuracy.

Photo: William Gottlieb

Photo: William Gottlieb

Charlie Parker

Other titles available in the In Session with Series

Guitar Collections

CARLOS SANTANA
All I Ever Wanted
Europa
Flor D'Luna
Hannibal
Samba Pa Ti
SensitiveKind
Order ref 6601A

PETER GREEN
Black Magic Woman
Merry Go Round
Need Your Love So Bad
Albatross
Watch Out
Man Of The World
Order ref 6602A

JEFF BECK
Jeff's Boogie (Beck's Boogie)
Led Boots
Starcycle
El Becko
Savoy
Big Block
Order ref 6604A

Guitar Collections

GEORGE BENSON
Breezin'
I Remember Wes
Lady
On Broadway
Valdez In The Country
The Wind And I
Order ref 6603A

CHUCK BERRY
Johnny B Goode
Maybellene
Memphis Tennessee
Roll Over, Beethoven
Too Much Monkey Business
No Particular Place To Go
Order ref 6606A

ROD STEWART
I Don't Want To Talk About It
Maggie May
Tonight's The Night
What Am I Gonna Do (I'm So In Love With You)
You Wear It Well
You're In My Heart
Order ref 6607A

Vocal Collection

THE DIVAS
Evergreen
Get Here
How Do I Live
I Will Always Love You
My Heart Will Go On
Respect
The Wind Beneath My Wings
We've Only Just Begun
Order ref 6611A